CUBAN
HOME COOKING

Favorite Recipes
From A
Cuban Home Kitchen

Seaside
Publishing

Seaside Publishing
687 Alderman Road #203
Palm Harbor, Florida 34683
1-888-Fla-Book (352-2665)

http://www.famousflorida.com

Manufactured in the United States of America

Editor: Joyce LaFray

Contributing Editor: Susan Sachs

Cover Illustration: Jane Tasciotti

Illustrations: Joan Croom

Library of Congress Number 89-060856

ISBN 0-942084-37-3

ACKNOWLEDGMENTS

I wish to express thanks to my husband, Evelio, for his patience in sampling and translating; to my mother-in-law, Bertha, for her helpful assistance; to my friend, Janet, for her willingness to type; to my publisher, Joyce LaFray Young and her staff for their devoted interest in publishing international cuisine; and especially for the recipe contributions of my husband's grandmother, Maria, who shared her many years of experience with me before recently passing away.

CUBAN HOME COOKING

The neighbors of Cuban families have long experienced the savory flavor of Cuban cuisine. Carried by a gentle breeze from house to house, the aroma frequently raises the question: "What is that you are cooking, and how can I make it?" This is usually answered "by adding a little of this and a pinch of that," and by naming ingredients that are not familiar to the questioner.

The combinations of spices used in Cuban cooking have a great similarity to those found in Spanish dishes, but the Cuban people have created many of their own unique tastes. The recipes in this cookbook represent some of the best homestyle recipes you'll find for truly delicious Cuban home-cooked meals. By following these simple recipes you can create authentic **Cuban Home Cooking.**

There are as many variations from cook to cook in the preparation of various Cuban dishes as there are ways to prepare American fried chicken or vegetable soup. Several of these recipes were developed by a Cuban friend of mine with more than 60 years of experience under her apron. She prepared Cuban food here in America just as it had been prepared in her homeland. Before the Cuban political changes in the 1960s, few canned goods were available in her Cuban homeland. Almost everything was bought fresh. Spices were dried, but herbs and vegetables were always fresh, as were meats and seafood. Most people shopped on a daily basis, visiting one market for meats, one for vegetables and another for seafood.

In Cuba, early in the morning, one could hear the Havana street vendors "hawking" their products as they moved along the avenues. Live chickens could be bought and dressed on the spot. Seafood was sold in a similar manner, or you could buy it in the plazas near the Port as the fishing boats proudly brought in their daily catch. At the port plaza, a quick lunch would consist of a plate of raw oysters, boiled shrimp or fried fish.

Continued

Cubans who arrived in America in the 1950s and 60s found few markets that sold their familiar vegetables, fruits, and special cuts of meat. Today, however, many Caribbean markets have opened, and adaptations have been made, some out of necessity, others out of convenience. For instance, in Cuba, olive oil and lard were generally used in cooking. On arriving here Cuban cooks found olive oil too expensive, and lard too difficult to find and not so healthful, so many began using other cooking oils.

American customs in eating have also been integrated into the Cuban culture. Breakfast in Cuba usually consisted of toasted Cuban bread (purchased as loaves similar to French bread) and Café con Leche (steaming hot milk mixed with sugar and Espresso coffee). Today, many still follow this custom, but others have grown to enjoy our breakfasts of eggs, ham and sausage, along with their Café con Leche.

Cuban Home Cooking introduces you to many dishes prepared in typical Cuban homes, with ingredients easily obtainable. Most items can be found in any local supermarket. Less common items can be located in a Cuban or Caribbean market. The convenient glossary offers some suggested substitutes, if necessary.

To accompany your meals, whether lunch or supper, you might add (just as many Cubans do) freshly baked Cuban bread, crisp crackers, and fruit pastries. A green salad almost always accompanies the meal. And don't forget the finishing touch, a demitasse of Cuban Espresso!

Enjoy your adventure into **Cuban Home Cooking!**

COMMONLY USED CUBAN FOODS
(With Their Spanish Translations)

almond . . . . almendra
bacon . . . . tocino
bay leaves (ground) . . . . laurel (molido)
beef . . . . carne de vaca
beef tail . . . . rabo de res
black (turtle) beans . . . . frijoles negros
butter . . . . mantequilla
carrot . . . . zanahoria
capers . . . . alcaparras finas
cassava . . . . yuca
cheese . . . . queso
chick peas . . . . garbanzos
chicken . . . . pollo
chicken breast . . . . pechuga
chicken leg quarters . . . . cuartos de muslos
chorizos . . . . chorizos
cinnamon . . . . cannela
coconut . . . . coco
collard greens . . . . berzas
condensed milk . . . . leche condensada
cumin (ground) . . . . comino (molido)
cracker meal . . . . galleta molida
dry white wine (usually sherry) . . . . vino seco
egg yolks . . . . yemas
eggs . . . . huevos
fish . . . . pescado
flank steak . . . . falda
garlic . . . . ajo
garlic powder . . . . ajo en polvo
great Northern beans . . . . judias blancas
grouper . . . . cherna
ham . . . . jamón
ham hock . . . . lacón
heel of round . . . . bola
liver . . . . higado

Continued

1

COMMONLY USED CUBAN FOODS
(With Their Spanish Translations)

milk . . . . leche
okra . . . . quimbombo
olive . . . . oliva, aceituna
olive oil . . . . aceite de oliva
onion . . . . cebolla
orange . . . . naranja
oregano (ground) . . . . oregano (molido)
parsley . . . . perejil
peas, green split . . . . chicharos
peas, small sweet . . . . petit-pois
pepper, black . . . . pimienta
pepper, green . . . . pimiento verde, ají verde
pepper, hot red . . . . guindilla
pepper, pimiento . . . . pimiento rojo
pepper, red sweet . . . . pimiento rojo
plantain . . . . platano
plantains, green . . . . platanos verdes
plantains, ripe . . . . platanos maduros
pork . . . . puerco, lechón
potato . . . . papa
rice . . . . arroz
salt . . . . sal
shrimp . . . . camarón
snapper . . . . pargo
sour orange . . . . naranja agria
sugar . . . . azucar
tomato . . . . tomate
tomato sauce . . . . salsa de tomate
top sirloin, thinly sliced . . . . palomilla
turnip . . . . nabo
vanilla . . . . vainilla
vermicelli, curly . . . . fideos
vermicelli, extra curly . . . . cabello de angel
wine . . . . vino

STOCKING THE SHELVES

The following is a list of items most commonly used in Cuban recipes. If you keep them on hand, you will only need to purchase those items pertaining to the particular recipe you are preparing.

cilantro/coriander

condiment of yellow coloring
(a brand name – "Bijol" or "Bija-Bekal," see glossary)

cracker meal, finely ground

fresh garlic

green bell peppers

ground and whole bay leaves

ground cumin

ground oregano

hot red dried peppers

fresh limes

olive oil, several Spanish varieties

onions

pimiento, jar or canned

plantains

potatoes

rice, regular long grain and Valencia-type short grain

saffron

sour or bitter oranges

sweet peas

tomato sauce

vinegar, several varieties, especially cider

RECIPE INDEX
(Listed According to Appearance)

5

CHICKEN SOUP
Sopa de Pollo

1¾	quarts water
½	chicken, cut into pieces
1	chicken liver
2	tablespoons minced garlic
1	teaspoon salt
¼	teaspoon ground oregano
1	medium onion, finely chopped
1	tablespoon tomato sauce
1	malanga*, peeled and chopped into 1-inch cubes
1	carrot, chopped
⅛	teaspoon yellow Bijol or Saffron condiment
2	ounces (about 1/5 of a 10-ounce package) extra Curly vermicelli
1	teaspoon lemon juice
	Lemon wedges for garnish

In a 3-quart pot, place water, chicken, chicken liver, garlic, salt, ground oregano, onion, and tomato sauce. Cook over medium-low heat until chicken is tender (about 30 minutes). Remove chicken from pot and bone it. Discard liver, fat and skin. Cut chicken into bite-size pieces. Return meat to the pot and add malanga (peeled and chopped) and carrots. Cook over medium-low heat until vegetables are tender (about 30 minutes.)

Using a potato masher, partially mash vegetables in pot, making sure to leave some larger pieces. Add yellow condiment and pasta (vermicelli). Cook until pasta is tender and mix in lemon juice just before serving. Serve lemon wedges on the side for each person to season to taste.

Serves 6.

*See Glossary.
You may substitute potato if necessary.

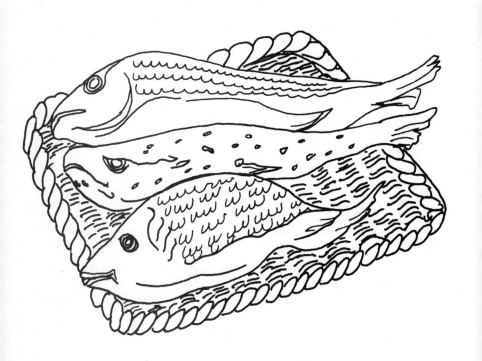

FISH SOUP
Sopa de Pescado

1½	quarts water
½	pound fresh white fish fillets
2	fish heads (or ½ pound fillets)
1	medium onion, finely chopped
1	green pepper, finely chopped
¼	cup tomato paste
¼	teaspoon Bijol or saffron
	Several sprigs of parsley
1	tablespoon minced garlic
1	teaspoon lemon juice
1	teaspoon dry white wine
	Dash of ground oregano
	Dash of ground pepper
¼	teaspoon vinegar
1	tablespoon pure Spanish olive oil
½	teaspoon salt or to taste
2	potatoes, peeled and chopped into 1-inch cubes
¼	pound dried bread, cut into 1-inch cubes
¼	cup pure Spanish olive oil

In a 3-quart pot, place all ingredients (except potatoes, bread, and ¼ cup olive oil). Bring to a boil and then cook over medium-low heat for 1½ hours or until liquid is reduced to about one-half the original amount. Pour the mixture through a sieve to remove all the bones and remains of the fish heads. Return fish meat to liquid, add potatoes and cook about 15 minutes. With a potato masher, partially mash potatoes.

In a separate pan, lightly brown the pieces of bread in heated olive oil and add them to the soup just before serving.

Serves 6.

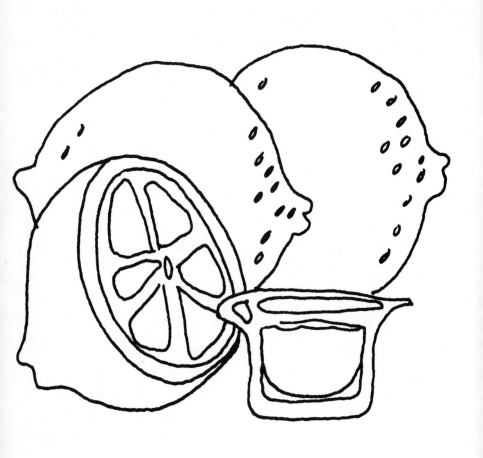

OKRA SOUP
Quimbombo

2   cups circular sliced okra, cut into ¼-inch slices
    Juice of 2 lemons
1   cup pork, cut into ½-inch cubes
½   green pepper, finely chopped
1   tablespoon minced fresh garlic
1   onion, finely chopped
¼   cup pure Spanish olive oil
½   cup tomato sauce
1   tablespoon cider vinegar
1   tablespoon dry Sherry wine
    Dash ground oregano
2   cups water (use water shrimp was boiled in)
1   peeled green plantain (not quite ripe)
    Cooking oil
½   cup shrimp, boiled, peeled and deveined, water reserved

In a large bowl, mix okra with lemon juice, cover with water and allow to soak for about 30 minutes. Drain and wash okra to remove the excess liquid substance covering okra.

In a deep frying pan, sauté pork, green pepper, garlic, and onion in olive oil until onions are translucent. Add the tomato sauce, vinegar, wine, and oregano. Cook about 2 minutes over medium heat. Add okra and water to pan and cook until okra is tender.

In a separate pan, boil plantain until it is tender enough to mash. Shape into small balls with a little cooking oil. Add plantain balls and shrimp to soup and cook for about 15 minutes.

Serves 4.

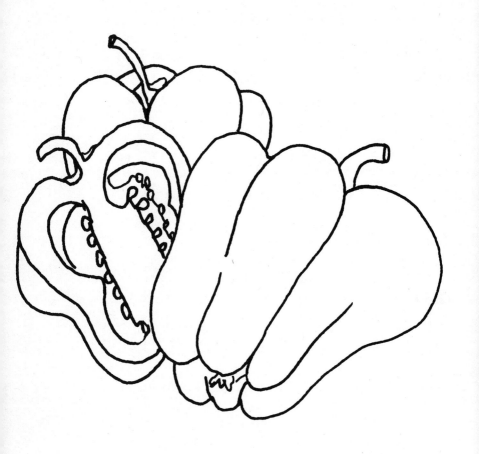

GALICIAN POTTAGE
Caldo Gallego

2	quarts water
1	cup dry white beans, pre-soaked
2	chorizos (Spanish sausage)
½	pound cured ham, chopped
	Several small pieces of pork fat
1	onion, finely chopped
1	tablespoon minced garlic
¼	cup chopped green pepper
1	tablespoon tomato sauce
1	tablespoon pure Spanish olive oil
¼	cup chopped turnip
1	potato, peeled and chopped into ½-inch cubes
1	cup chopped collard greens

Place all ingredients (except potatoes and collard greens) in a 3-quart pot. Cook on medium-low heat until beans are tender (about 3 hours). Add potato pieces and collard greens and cook until tender. Salt to taste.

Serves 8.

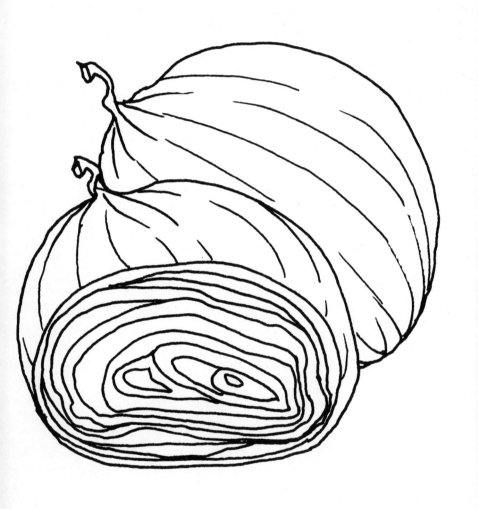

SPANISH BEAN SOUP
Guiso de Garbanzos

1	cup chick peas, pre-soaked overnight
2	ounces chorizos (Spanish sausage)
4	cups water
½	teaspoon salt
1	smoked ham hock
2	tablespoons crushed garlic
3	tablespoons tomato sauce
	Chopped ham
1	tablespoon chopped green bell pepper
½	teaspoon ground oregano
½	teaspoon cider vinegar
2	tablespoons pure Spanish olive oil
½	cup finely chopped onions
1	cup calabaza squash*
	broken, or cut into chunks
⅓	head cabbage, leaves separated
1	potato, peeled and chopped into 1-inch cubes

In a 3-quart pot, place all of the ingredients (except for calabaza, cabbage and potato). Cook over medium-low heat until peas are tender, about 2 hours. Add the last three ingredients and cook until they are soft. Add the chopped ham and blend well.

Serves 4.

*See glossary. May substitute pumpkin.

SPLIT PEA SOUP
Guiso de Chicharos

1   12-ounce package dried green split peas (about 1½ cups)
1¼   quarts water
1   teaspoon pure Spanish olive oil
½   teaspoon ground oregano
¼   teaspoon ground cumin
1   smoked ham hock
1   cup calabaza squash*
1   potato, peeled and chopped into cubes
4   teaspoons tomato sauce
1   teaspoon cider vinegar
⅓   cup chopped onion
1   teaspoon minced fresh garlic
¼   cup chopped green pepper
1   tablespoon pure Spanish olive oil
     Salt to taste

Rinse peas. Combine all ingredients (except onion, garlic, green pepper and 1 tablespoon olive oil) in a 2-quart saucepan. Cover and cook over medium-low heat until peas are tender.

In a separate pan, sauté onion, garlic and green pepper in the tablespoon of olive oil, then add to soup. Simmer for about 20 minutes. Salt to taste.

Serves 6.

*See glossary.

SALAD
Ensalada

In Cuban home meals, salads have customarily been refreshing and uncomplicated additions to menus. The following offers two variations to the salad as a nice addition to your meal.

SALAD PLATTER
Fuente de Ensalada

1 head of Boston lettuce
1 tomato, sliced
1 onion, thinly sliced
6 asparagus spears, canned and preferably white
¼ cup sweet green peas, cooked and chilled
¼ cup snap beans, cooked and chilled
  Apple cider vinegar
  Spanish Extra Virgin olive oil

Wash and dry lettuce leaves thoroughly and cover a large platter with them. Arrange the tomato, onion, asparagus, peas and beans attractively over the lettuce. Sprinkle salad with a little vinegar and olive oil.

Serves 4.

AVOCADO AND ONION
Aguacate y Cebolla

1 large or 2 small avocados
1 onion, thinly sliced into rings
  Cider vinegar
  Spanish Extra Virgin olive oil

Peel and slice avocado in about ½ to 1-inch wedges and place 3 pieces sideways on each individual plate. Place a few onion rings over the top and serve with vinegar and olive oil at the table.

Serves 4.

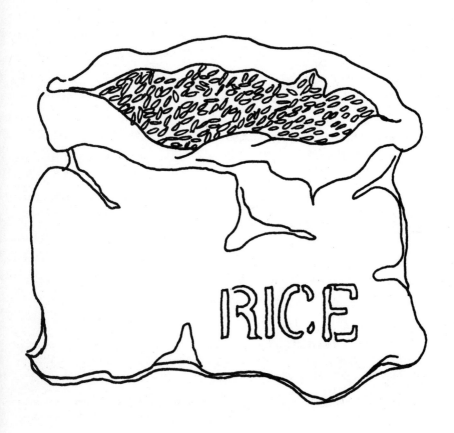

WHITE RICE
Arroz Blanco

2   cups long-grain rice
3   cups water
1   tablespoon cooking oil
¼   teaspoon salt or more to taste
1   tablespoon fresh lime juice (optional)

Place rice, water, cooking oil, and salt in a heavy-bottomed saucepan (about 2- or 3-quart capacity) and bring to a boil. Reduce heat to low, cover and simmer for about 25 minutes or until all the water is absorbed and rice is tender but not mushy. Turn off heat, add lime juice (if desired), and stir rice with a fork to fluff it up. Let stand covered about 15 minutes before serving.

Serves 4.

CASSAVA
Yuca

4-6   fresh cassavas, peeled and halved, OR
1   20-ounce package frozen cassava
1   teaspoon salt
4   garlic cloves, minced
1   lemon, juice of
½   cup pure Spanish olive oil

Place cassava in large pot and cover with water. Add salt. Boil cassava until very tender (about 30 minutes). Drain off water and set cassava aside. Sprinkle minced garlic over the cassava and add juice of the lemon. In a separate small pan, heat olive oil until it begins to bubble. Pour it immediately over the cassava and gently mix. Serve immediately.

Serves 4.

Cassava is especially good as an accompaniment to roast pork and moros (black beans and rice cooked together).

Serves 6-8.

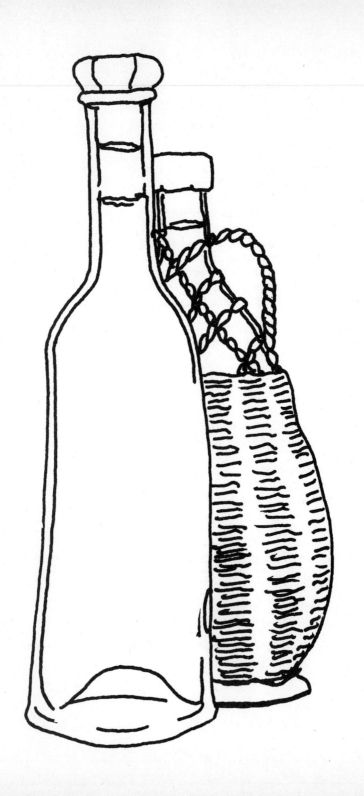

BLACK BEANS
Frijoles Negros
(Allow Time For Beans To Soak Overnight)

1   14-ounce package dried black beans
2   quarts water
⅛   teaspoon baking soda
½   teaspoon ground oregano
2   teaspoons cumin
1   green pepper, cleaned and cut into quarters
½   onion, finely chopped
2   tablespoons minced fresh garlic
¼   cup pure Spanish olive oil
3   tablespoons cider vinegar
¼   cup dry white Sherry wine
1   teaspoon salt
1½ teaspoon cumin
6   cups cooked white rice

Rinse beans and discard any stones and debris. In a large pot, soak beans overnight in water with baking soda, oregano, cumin, and green pepper.

The next day cook beans in the same water on medium-low heat for about 3 hours or until the beans are very tender and liquid is reduced, and somewhat thickened. Make sure liquid in pot does not entirely boil away. To prevent beans from burning, add more water when necessary.

In a small pan, sauté onion and garlic in olive oil until onion is translucent and begins to brown. Add several large spoonfuls of the black beans to this mixture and stir, simmering several minutes. Return this mixture of onions and black beans to the large pot of beans. Mix well and add vinegar, wine, salt and remaining cumin. Cook another 20 minutes. Serve over white rice on individual plates or in individual side bowls.

Serves 6.

BLACK BEANS AND RICE
Moros

Black bean recipe
3 6-inch pieces of slab bacon
2 cloves fresh garlic, crushed
2 tablespoons pure Spanish olive oil
1 cup liquid from previously made black beans
(or use water to make up cup if necessary)
1 cup uncooked white rice
½ cup water
½ cup cooked and drained black beans
½ teaspoons pure Spanish olive oil

Prepare Black Beans recipe on page 23. Reserve liquid from beans.

In a 2-quart saucepan, sauté the slab bacon and garlic in olive oil until they are lightly browned. Remove from pan and set aside. Place rice in the pan and cook until it begins to crackle. Add water and liquid from soaking of black beans. Cover and cook over medium-low heat until rice is rather dry (water will be almost completely absorbed) and almost tender. Add black beans and olive oil and cook a little longer until rice is tender but not too soft or mushy. Mix in browned pieces of bacon and garlic.

Serves 4.

FRIED GREEN PLANTAINS
Plátanos Verdes Fritos

Unripe plantains (1 per person)
Pure Spanish olive oil
Salt to taste

Choose a plantain with a yellow-green or all-green peel that is hard to the touch. Remove peel and slice in about 1-inch perpendicular slices. If it is too difficult to remove the peel, first cut off the ends and then make 4 end-to-end cuts through the peel only and gently lift and roll off the peel.

Heat oil in sauté pan to medium-high. Place plantain slices, cut side down, in oil and cook 1 minute on each side until pieces are slightly soft but not brown. Remove slices and press individually between two pieces of clean brown paper until somewhat flattened. Return plantain to pan and cook on both sides until they are lightly browned. Salt to taste. Serve instead of bread.

Yield: 1 plantain per person.

FRIED SWEET PLANTAINS
Plátanos Maduros Fritos

Ripe plantains* (1 per person)
Pure Spanish olive oil

Select very ripe plantains,with a partially black or all black peel and a little soft to the touch. Remove the peel and slice the plantain obliquely, or in a slant, in about 1-inch slices.

Heat cooking oil to medium heat and fry the plantain slices on their cut surface. Oil should cover at least one-half of the plantain. Fry until golden brown on each side. Remove from pan and place on clean brown paper to drain excess oil. They may be served with almost any meal.

Yield: 1 plantain per person.

*See Glossary.

CALABAZA FRITTERS

1½   pounds calabaza*
2   tablespoons butter
1   egg
1   cup sugar
¼   teaspoon nutmeg
¼   teaspoon cinnamon
1½   cups self-rising flour
     Cooking oil

Peel calabaza, cut into chunks and boil in a large pot of water until very tender. Drain off water, mash calabaza and drain again. Mix 1½ cups of mashed calabaza together with butter, egg, and sugar.

Sift flour with nutmeg and cinnamon and add to calabaza mixture. Mix well and drop by spoonfuls into heated cooking oil that just almost covers the fritters. Cook on both sides until lightly browned. Serve immediatly.

Yield: 12 fritters.

*See glossary.

BAKED SWEET PLANTAINS IN WINE
Plátanos a la Tentación

4   ripe plantains
1   cup pure Spanish olive oil
½   cup white or brown sugar
½   teaspoon cinnamon
1   cup unsalted white Sherry wine

Preheat oven to 350°F. Select well-ripened plantains and remove peel. Slice them lengthwise in half. In a large sauté pan, heat oil to medium and add plantain slices, cooking them until lightly browned on each side.

Place them in a large baking dish and sprinkle the sugar over all. Add cinnamon and cover with wine. Bake for 30 minutes or until they take on a reddish hue.

Serves 4.

GARDEN EGGS
Huevos a la Jardinera

½   cup fully cooked chopped imported ham
1   cup Sofrito (see page 87)
½   cup small green peas
4-6 fresh eggs
½   cup grated Parmesan cheese
2   tablespoons cracker meal
    Pure Spanish olive oil
    Garnish of canned pimiento strips (optional)

Preheat oven to 350°F. In a medium-size saucepan, lightly brown ham in cooking oil. Remove from heat. Mix ham, Sofrito, and peas together. Pour half of the mixture into the bottom of a 1½-quart baking dish.

Crack eggs and drop gently one at a time on top of the sauce. Spoon rest of sauce over eggs. Sprinkle cheese and cracker meal over the surface. Bake for about 15 minutes or until eggs are as cooked as you like. Garnish with pimiento strips, if desired. Serve with white rice and fried sweet plantains.

Serves 2-3.

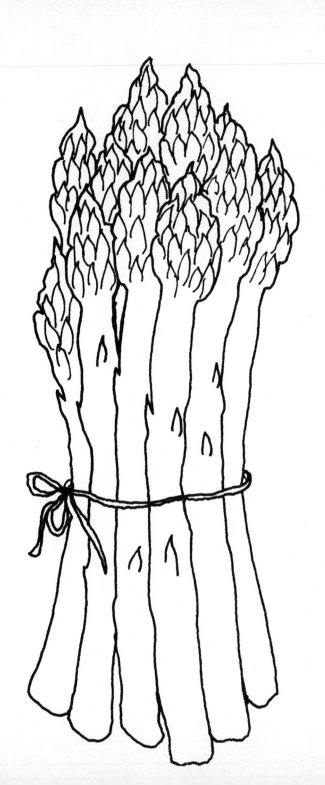

CHICKEN SALAD
Ensalada de Pollo

1   chicken, cut into pieces
1   tablespoon dry white wine
½   onion, finely chopped
4   garlic cloves, crushed and minced
     Juice of ½ lemon
¼   teaspoon oregano
1   large potato, cubed
¼   head lettuce, chopped (reserve several large leaves)
3   hard-boiled eggs (1 sliced)
¼   cup pimiento, chopped
¼   cup pimiento, strips (for garnish)
¼   cup cooked English peas
1   tablespoon fresh lemon juice
¼   cup mayonnaise
¼   teaspoon vinegar
1   apple, chopped
     White asparagus spears, canned
     Pinch of salt

In a large covered pot, boil chicken until tender in water with wine, onion, garlic, lemon juice, and oregano. Remove chicken and allow to cool. Remove meat from bones and refrigerate. Cook potato cubes in water with a pinch of salt until soft.

Set aside larger leaves of the lettuce and chop remainder of lettuce into small pieces. Chop chicken meat into small pieces as well as 2 eggs, and ¼ cup pimiento. Mix these with chopped lettuce, potato cubes, peas, lemon juice, mayonnaise, vinegar, and chopped apple. Use enough mayonnaise so mixture holds together well.

Arrange large lettuce leaves on a platter and place the mound of chicken salad on top. Decorate with pimiento strips, asparagus and remaining egg, which has been sliced.

Serves 6.

CHICKEN CROQUETTES
Croquetas de Pollo

3   chicken breasts (enough to yield 1½ cups of ground chicken)
¼   cup all-purpose flour
¾   cup milk
1   tablespoon butter or margarine
3   tablespoons cracker meal
½   teaspoon garlic salt
    Dash pepper
1   tablespoon dry white wine
2   eggs, well-beaten
    Finely ground cracker meal, salted to taste
    Oil for deep frying

In a large pot, boil chicken until tender, then drain water and allow chicken to cool. Remove meat from bones and grind chicken in a meat grinder or blender. Set chicken aside in large bowl.

Place the flour in a large sauté pan and slowly add milk, stirring constantly over medium heat. Add butter and continue to stir until it reaches paste-like consistency. Remove from heat and stir in 3 tablespoons of cracker meal, salt, pepper and garlic. Sprinkle chicken with wine and add flour mixture. Mix well and refrigerate.

After mixture is thoroughly chilled, make finger-sized croquettes. Rubbing a small amount of vegetable oil in the palm of your hand helps keep mixture from sticking. Dip each croquette first in the egg, then the cracker meal, then the egg and then a final coating of cracker meal. Deep-fry several minutes until golden brown, but do not overcook.

Yield: 15-20 croquettes.

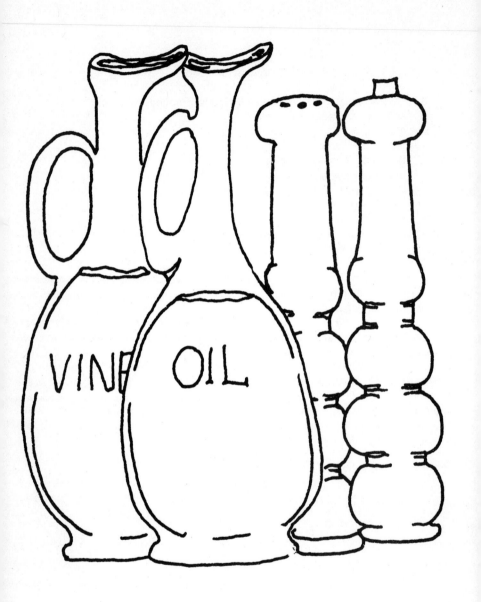

CHICKEN AND YELLOW RICE
Arroz con Pollo

1	chicken, cut into pieces and slightly browned (or 4 chicken breasts with skin and fat removed)
3	cups water
¾	teaspoon salt
1	tablespoon tomato sauce
1	onion, finely chopped
1	teaspoon pure Spanish olive oil
1	green bell pepper, cut into quarters
½	red bell pepper, cut into quarters
1	tablespoon minced fresh garlic
½	teaspoon ground cumin
½	teaspoon ground oregano
1	tablespoon dry white Sherry or other white wine
1	tablespoon cider vinegar
¼	teaspoon Bijol* or saffron
1-2	cans beer
1½	cups medium-short grain Valencia rice
½	cup sweet peas, pre-cooked
	Canned pimiento strips
	Canned white asparagus spears
	Cooked sweet peas

In a 4-6 quart pot, combine chicken (which has been browned in a small amount of cooking oil), water, salt, tomato sauce, onion, olive oil, green pepper, red pepper, garlic, ground cumin, ground oregano, wine, vinegar, and saffron or Bijol to color rice yellow. Cook until chicken is tender, about 30-40 minutes.

Remove chicken and set aside Add enough beer to liquid in the pot to make a total of 5 cups. Add rice and cook on medium to medium-low heat, stirring occasionally until rice is tender. Add more beer or water, if necessary, as rice should be moist. Mix in chicken and about ¼ cup of the peas.

Turn out on a platter and garnish with asparagus spears, pimiento strips and juice, and remainder of the sweet peas.

Serves 3-4.

*See glossary.

FRIED CHICKEN, CUBAN STYLE
Pollo Frito, Estilo Cubano
(Allow 1 Hour to Marinate)

1	chicken, cut into pieces
5-6	cloves fresh garlic, crushed
½	teaspoon ground oregano
½	onion, sliced into rings
¼	cup sour orange juice (or ⅛ orange juice and ⅛ lime juice)
1	tablespoon dry white Sherry or other white wine
¼	teaspon salt
	Pure Spanish olive oil
	Fresh parsley

Remove skin and fat from chicken pieces, pierce meat in several places with long fork prongs, and place chicken in a bowl. Combine garlic, oregano, onion, orange juice, wine and salt. Pour mixture over chicken. Cover and marinate in the refrigerator for about 1 hour.

Remove chicken pieces from marinade, pat dry and fry them in olive oil until they are golden brown. Place chicken on serving platter and keep warm. Remove garlic and onion rings from marinade and brown them with oil in a separate pan. Sprinkle garlic and onion over chicken. Add fresh parsley.

Serves 4.

POT ROASTED CHICKEN
Pollo Asado

1   chicken, cut into pieces
¼   teaspoon salt
2   teaspoons fresh garlic, minced
2   tablespoons pure Spanish olive oil
1   medium onion, sliced into rings
2   tablespoons sour orange juice (or 1 T. orange and 1 T. lime juice)
½   cup dry white wine
¼   teaspoon oregano
1   bay leaf
     Water to cover
     Salt to taste

Remove skin and fat from chicken and sprinkle chicken pieces with salt and 1 teaspoon of garlic. In a large pot, brown chicken in oil over medium heat. Add onion and cook until it begins to brown. Now add juice, wine, remaining garlic, oregano, and bay leaf. Add enough water to pot to just cover chicken and reduce liquid until it practically disappears and the chicken begins to fry again. Salt to taste.

Serves 4.

ROAST PORK
Lechón Asado
(Allow Time To Marinate)

1	3-pound pork roast
2	tablespoons minced fresh garlic
½	teaspoon salt
¼	cup sour orange juice (or ⅛ cup orange, ⅛ cup lime juice)
¼	teaspoon ground black pepper
¼	teaspoon ground bay leaves
½	teaspoon ground oregano
½	teaspoon ground cumin
1	tablespoon pure Spanish olive oil ·
	Mojo (see page 85)

Remove excess fat and all of the skin from pork roast. Pierce meat in several areas and marinate roast in a mixture of garlic, salt, juice, pepper, bay leaves, oregano, cumin, and olive oil for at least 1 hour.

Place roast in a pan with the fat side up, and reserve marinade for basting. Roast at 350° F. for about 2½ hours or until a meat thermometer registers 170° F. and the meat is browned.

Turn the meat and baste frequently with marinade while cooking. If drippings begin to smoke or burn, add a little water to the drippings in the pan. After meat is well done, remove from oven and allow to cool before cutting into thick slices. Serve with "Mojo," black beans, white rice, and fried sweet or green plantains.

Serves 4.

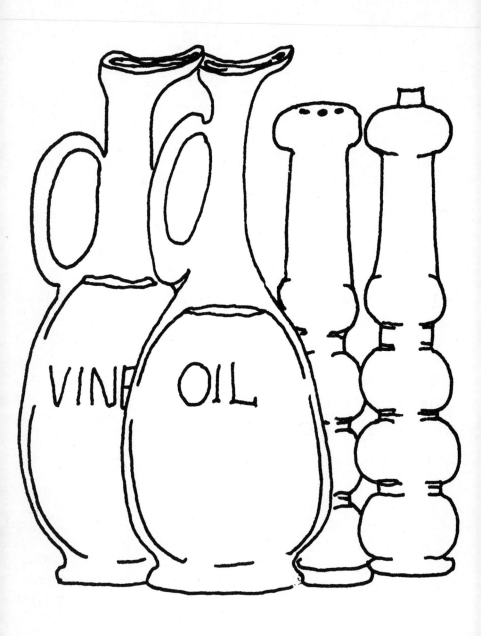

FRIED PORK CHUNKS
Masas de Puerco Fritas
(Allow Time To Marinate Overnight)

1   2½-pound fresh pork loin
12   garlic cloves, peeled and crushed
½   large onion, chopped
½   cup sour orange juice (or ¼ cup orange, ¼ cup lime juice)
½   cup pure Spanish olive oil
½   teaspoon salt
     Oil for deep frying
½   fresh onion, sliced into rings
4   lime wedges with rind

Cut pork into 1- or 2-inch chunks removing most of the fat. To prepare the marinade, mix together garlic, chopped onion, juice, olive oil, and salt. Pour marinade over the pork chunks and marinate for several hours (preferably overnight) in the refrigerator.

Remove meat from marinade and deep fry in cooking oil until well done. Garnish with fresh onion slices and lime wedges.

Serves 4.

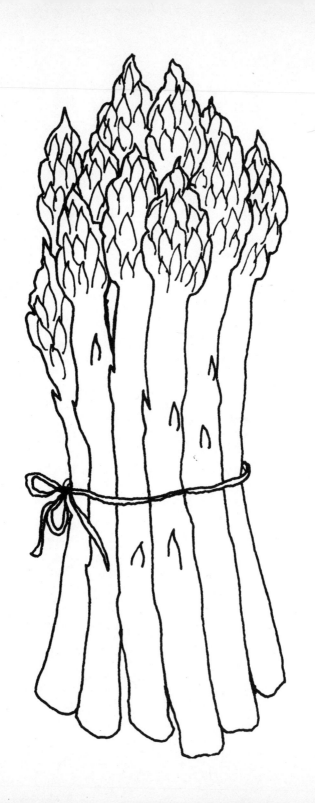

SPANISH BEEF STEW
Carne con Papas

1 pound top round, cubed
  Olive oil for sautéing
2 teaspoons salt
1 teaspoon black pepper
1 clove garlic, crushed
1 20-ounce can whole tomatoes, crushed
1 large Spanish onion, chopped
1 green bell pepper, chopped
2 tablespoons oregano
3 whole bay leaves
3 medium potatoes, peeled and cubed
3 tablespoons flour
¼ cup water
4 carrots, peeled and sliced into rounds
1 1-pound can whole string beans

Place olive oil in a large deep skillet or dutch oven with the top round, salt, pepper and garlic. Brown well. Add tomatoes, onion and green pepper. Cook for a few minutes longer.

Add oregano and bay leaves and bring to a boil. Reduce heat to a slow simmer. Cook for about 30 minutes longer.

Add potatoes, carrots, and string beans and cook until meat and vegetables are tender, about 30 minutes.

Mix flour and water together to make a smooth roux. Add to stew. Stir and cook until thickened.

From THE LINCOLN RESTAURANT, TAMPA, FLORIDA

Serves 4.

HOT OXTAIL STEW
Rabo Encendido

2	pounds beef tail, cut into pieces
1	pound beef stew meat
1	teaspoon salt
½	teaspoon black pepper
	Pure Spanish olive oil for sautéing
1	quart water
1	teaspoon minced garlic
¼	teaspoon oregano
½	green pepper, chopped
1	onion, chopped
2	fresh tomatoes, chopped
1	9-ounce can whole tomatoes
2	ounces chorizo sausage, cut into pieces
1	tablespoon capers
¼	cup raisins
2-3	cups potatoes, chopped into 1-inch pieces
	Hot red pepper sauce* to taste

Sprinkle tail pieces and stew meat with salt and pepper and brown in cooking oil in a large pot or dutch oven. Add water, garlic, oregano, green pepper, onion, and tomatoes and cook over medium heat for approximately 1 hour, or until meat is tender.

Add chorizo, capers, raisins and potatoes and continue to cook until potatoes are tender. Mash about one-half of the potatoes to thicken the liquid. Season to taste with red pepper sauce. Cook over low heat another 15 minutes. Serve with white rice and fried sweet plantains.

Serves 4.

*Louisiana Hot Sauce is a good choice, or use homemade.

ITALIAN LIVER CUBAN STYLE
Hígado a la Italiana

1   onion, sliced into rings
3   teaspoons fresh minced garlic
1   green bell pepper, thinly sliced lengthwise
3   tablespoons pure Spanish olive oil
1   pound beef or calves liver, sliced into ½-inch wide strips 1½ inches long
¼   teaspoon ground oregano
½   teaspoon ground cumin
½   teaspoon salt to taste
¾   cup dry white wine
2   tablespoons cider vinegar

Prepare this recipe no more than 30 minutes in advance. Sauté the onion, garlic and green bell pepper in olive oil until onion begins to become translucent.

Drain liver strips and add to the sautéed vegetables, cooking about 5 minutes on medium-high heat. Sprinkle liver with the other ingredients, mix well, and cook another 1-2 minutes. Serve with white rice.

Serves 4.

SHREDDED BEEF
Ropa Vieja*

1   pound flank steak
2   quarts water or more
1   carrot, chopped
1   onion, chopped
4   cloves garlic, crushed
½   green bell pepper, sliced lengthwise
1½ cup Sofrito (see page 87)
½   cup meat broth (water reserved from cooking steak)
1   tablespoon dry white Sherry or other white wine
¼   cup cooked sweet peas
1   2-ounce jar pimiento strips
     Salt to taste
¼   cup toasted bread squares

Boil meat in a 4-quart pot with about 2 quarts of water, with the carrot, onion, garlic, and green bell pepper, for about 15 minutes. Reduce heat to medium-low, cover, and cook for about 2 hours or until meat is tender and well done.

Remove meat and allow to cool. Pound the meat, fraying the meat fibers until you have very thread-like strips. Place it in a pan with Sofrito, broth, the cooked carrot, wine, and peas. Salt to taste and cook for about 5 minutes. Pour in the juice from the jar of pimiento. Add a few of the strips and mix.

Arrange meat on a platter with the remaining pimiento strips placed on top, along with the toasted bread squares. Accompany with white rice, fried sweet plantains, and black beans.

Serves 3-4.

*The literal translation is "old clothes."

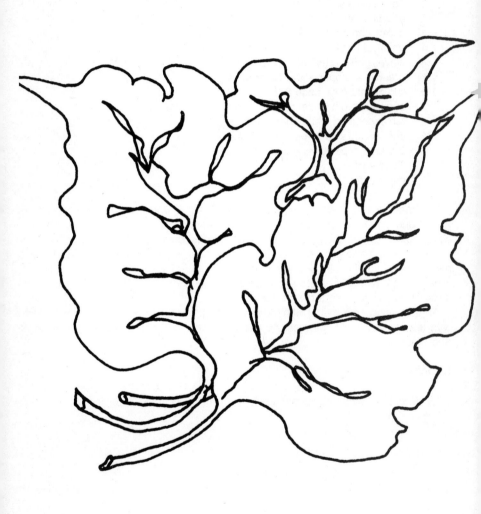

FRIED STEAK
Bistec Frito
(Allow Time To Marinate)

4	top sirloin or palomilla steaks (about ¼ to ½ inch thick)
1	tablespoon fresh minced garlic
2	tablespoons sour orange juice (or 1 T. orange, 1 T. lime juice)
1	onion, sliced into rings
¼	teaspoon salt
½	cup finely chopped onion
½	cup finely chopped fresh parsley
¼	cup pure Spanish olive oil

Place steaks in a shallow pan and sprinkle with minced garlic, juice, onion rings, and salt. Cover steaks and marinate in the refrigerator about 30 minutes before frying.

Heat oil in a frying pan to medium or medium-high. Fry steaks one or two at a time (with a share of the onion rings) until they are browned.

Serve with a side dish of the uncooked chopped onion and parsley mixed together, to be sprinkled over the steak as desired.

Serves 4.

*Cubans generally use a cut of steak called "palomilla."

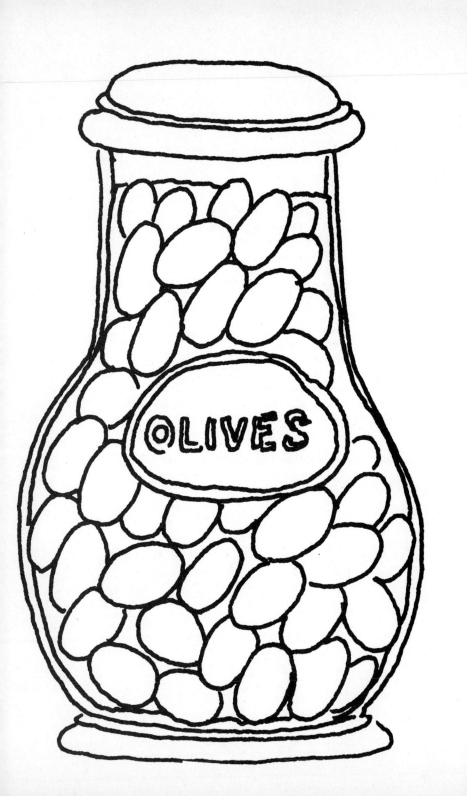

BRAISED STEAK
Bistec en Cazuela
(Allow Time To Marinate)

1½   pounds top round or palomilla steaks, about ¼ inch thick
1   green bell pepper, sliced lengthwise into ¼-inch-wide strips
1   onion, sliced into thin rings
¼   cup sour orange juice (or ⅛ cup orange, ⅛ cup lime juice)
1   teaspoon minced garlic
⅛   teaspoon salt or to taste
⅛   teaspoon ground cumin
¼   cup dry white Sherry or other white wine
2   tablespoons pure Spanish olive oil

Divide steak into 4 large or 8 smaller pieces, and place in a shallow pan. Combine remaining ingredients (except oil) and mix with the steaks. Cover and refrigerate for about 1 hour.

Remove steaks and fry them in the oil until they are lightly browned. Pour all the liquid and vegetables over steaks and cook slowly until meat is very tender, adding a little water if necessary.

Serves 4.

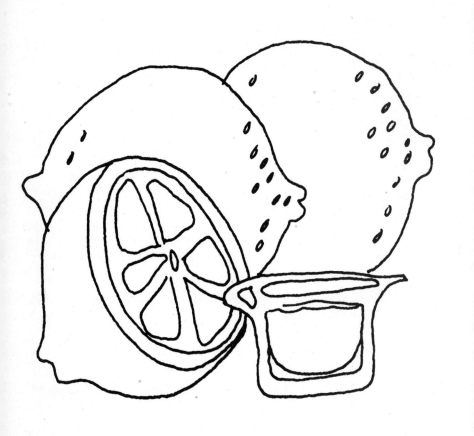

BREADED STEAK
Bistec Empanizado

4   steaks, ¼-inch thick, top round or cube steak
½   cup chopped onion
1   tablespoon minced fresh garlic
¼   cup sour orange juice (or ⅛ cup orange, ⅛ cup lime juice)
¼   teaspoon salt
4   eggs, well-beaten
1   cup finely ground cracker meal, salted to taste
1   lime cut into wedges
½   onion sliced into rings
    Pure Spanish olive oil

Sprinkle steaks with chopped onion, garlic, juice, and salt. Rub garlic into meat. Marinate for a few hours in the refrigerator. Brush off the onion pieces and dip each steak in the egg first and then cracker meal, coating each steak completely. Fry steaks in cooking oil on medium heat until golden brown and well done. Serve with lime wedges and a few sliced raw onion rings.

Serves 4.

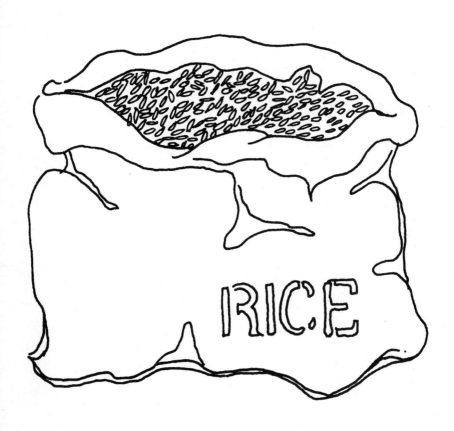

BEEF ROAST CUBAN STYLE
Carne Asada

2-3	pounds eye of round roast
¼	pound ham
1	carrot
1	teaspoon minced garlic
1	teaspoon ground oregano
1	teaspoon vinegar
1	tablespoons sour orange juice (or ½ T. orange and ½ T. lime juice)
½	cup dry white wine plus 1 tablespoon
1	onion. sliced into rings
3	bay leaves
2	tablespoons or more pure Spanish olive oil
	Several small white peeled potatoes

Cubans often stuff the center of the roast with ham and carrots. To do this, make an opening down the center of the roast with a sharp skewer and stuff before marinating. Pierce entire roast with long fork prongs and marinate meat in refrigerator for at least an hour in the mixture of garlic, ground oregano, vinegar, orange juice, wine, onion, and bay leaves.

Remove meat from marinade and pat dry. Heat cooking oil in a large pot and brown roast, starting with the ends. After the roast is browned, add marinade to the pot and add enough water to bring liquid up until it half covers the meat. Bring to a boil and then reduce temperature to medium-low. Cover and cook roast for 1 hour on one side and then turn and cook for about 1 hour on the other side. Add more water if necessary so liquid continues to cover about half the meat. Cook until roast is very tender.

About 15 minutes before the end of cooking time, add several small peeled white potatoes and another tablespoon of wine. Simmer and reduce liquid, leaving a small amount for gravy. Serve with black beans, rice, and fried sweet plantains.

Serves 4.

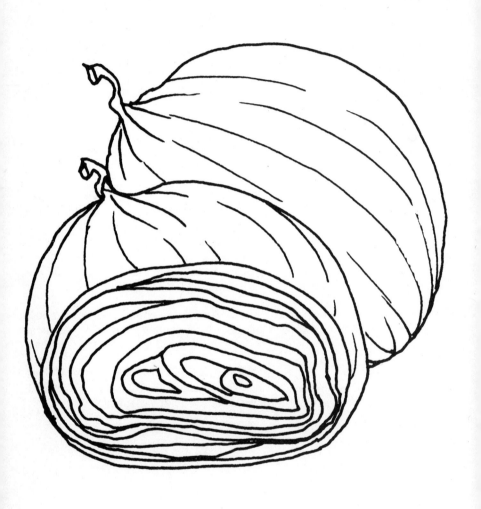

BEEF AND POTATOES
Carne con Papas

2   pounds beef round, or beef for kabobs
⅛   teaspoon ground oregano
½   teaspoon ground cumin
1   tablespoon minced fresh garlic
1   tablespoon plus 1 teaspoon of vinegar
1   tablespoon dry white Sherry or other white wine
½   onion, chopped
½   green bell pepper, finely chopped
2   tablespoons pure Spanish olive oil or more
3   cups water
¼   cup tomato sauce
1   large potato, chopped into small pieces
1   large carrot, chopped into several pieces
½   cup cut fresh green beans
2   tablespoons dry white Sherry or other white wine
¼   cup raisins, pre-soaked in warm water
12 green Manzanilla Spanish olives
    Salt to taste

Remove any excess fat from meat and cut into 1-inch cubes. Prepare marinade by combining oregano, cumin, garlic, vinegar, wine, onion and green pepper, and pour over meat while turning the cubes. Cover and refrigerate for at least 1 hour.

Remove meat, saving the marinade. In large pot, heat olive oil on medium-high heat and brown cubes on all sides. Add marinade to meat plus 3 cups of water and tomato sauce. Cover and cook over medium heat for about 45 minutes until meat is tender. Do not let liquid completely cook away; add more water if necessary.

Add potato, carrot, green beans, and enough water to cover half the meat and vegetables. Cook until meat is tender and liquid has been reduced to a small amount of sauce. The vegetables should also be tender. Add wine, raisins, and olives. Salt to taste. Serve with white rice and fried sweet plantains.

Serves 4.

MEAT HASH
Picadillo

1	pound ground chuck
3	tablespoons fat drippings from fried bacon
¼	pound ground ham
½	cup chopped onion
1	tablespoon minced fresh garlic
¼	cup chopped green bell pepper
	Dash oregano
1¼	teaspoons ground cumin
2	tablespoons tomato sauce
½	teaspoon vinegar
1	potato, chopped into ¼-½ inch cubes
¼	cup raisins
¼	cup chopped olives with pimiento
1	teaspoon capers
4	eggs, cooked sunny-side-up

Cook ground chuck in bacon drippings until it begins to brown, separating it so no chunks remain. Drain off all excess fat. Add ham, onion, garlic, and green pepper and cook until onions are translucent. Add oregano, cumin, tomato sauce and vinegar to meat and mix well.

In a separate pan, fry potato pieces until they are brown and add them to the meat along with raisins, olives, and capers. Place a sunny-side-up egg over the rice. Serve immediately with white rice and fried sweet plantains.

Serves 4.

MEAT BALLS
Albóndigas

2   cups ground chuck
¼   cup finely chopped onion
2   teaspoons minced garlic
1   egg
2   tablespoons flour
1   teaspoon oregano
¼   teaspoon cumin
¼   teaspoon salt
     Flour for coating
     Pure Spanish olive oil

Combine all ingredients (except flour) to form into nine meatballs and coat them with the flour. In a deep skillet, brown the meatballs in a small amount of heated cooking oil. Prepare the sauce (recipe follows) and add it to the meatballs. Reduce sauce until it is the consistency of light gravy. Serve with white rice and fried sweet plantains.

Serves 3.

Sauce for Meat Balls
Salsa para Albóndigas

½   cup onions, chopped
2   tablespoons green bell pepper, finely chopped
1   teaspoon minced garlic
2   tablespoons pure Spanish olive oil
½   cup tomato sauce
2   teaspoons vinegar
¼   teaspoon ground oregano
½   teaspoon crushed bay leaves
1   cup water
¼   cup dry white wine

In a saucepan, sauté onions, garlic, and green pepper in olive oil over medium heat until the onions are translucent. Add remainder of ingredients and mix well. Add to meat balls.

Serves 6-8.

MEAT LOAF
Pulpeta

¾   pound ground beef
¼   pound ground fully cooked ham
4   raw eggs
3   hard-boiled eggs
⅛   teaspoon salt
¼   teaspoon pepper
1   teaspoon oregano
1   teaspoon cumin
1   tablespoon minced garlic
½   teaspoon minced garlic
1¾   cups cracker meal
20   Manzanilla pimiento-stuffed olives
2   tablespoons pure Spanish olive oil

Thoroughly mix the beef and ham together and add 2 beaten eggs, salt, pepper, oregano, cumin, garlic and onion. Mix well. Add enough cracker meal (about ¾ cup) to make the meat hold its shape, and then form mixture into one large loaf (or two small loaves, if you desire).

Open the large loaf by cuttting in half horizontally. Place 3 hard-boiled eggs down the center and line the olives up on both sides. Tightly close the loaf again. Roll loaf in the other 2 beaten eggs and then cracker meal alternately 2-3 times, finishing up with the cracker meal. In a large skillet, brown loaf in the heated oil starting with the ends of the loaf.

After the loaf is browned, prepare the sauce (recipe follows). Pour sauce over the loaf and simmer for about 45 minutes, turning carefully once or twice. (If desired, you may bake in a preheated 350°F. oven.)

After loaf is well done, remove from heat and allow to cool before slicing. Garnish with parsley sprigs.

Sauce for Meat Loaf
Salsa Para Pulpeta

½   teaspoon minced garlic
¼   teaspoon oregano
¼   teaspoon ground bay leaves
2   tablespoons tomato sauce
½   cup white wine
   Parsley sprigs

Combine garlic, oregano, bay leves, tomato sauce ad wine. Mix well.

Serves 4-6.

MEAT STUFFED GREEN PEPPERS
Aji Relleno

6   medium green bell peppers
1   pound lean ground beef
½   pound fully cooked ground smoked ham
1   onion, finely chopped
1   teaspoon fresh minced garlic
1   teaspoon oregano
½   teaspoon black pepper
½   teaspoon ground cumin
¼   teaspoon salt
2   eggs
2   tablespoons flour
2   tablespoons pure Spanish olive oil
    Cooked white rice for 6 persons

Sauce

1   tablespoon olive oil
2   crushed garlic cloves
2   tablespoons chopped onion
1   8-ounce can tomato sauce
¼   cup dry white wine
¼   cup water
¼   teaspoon oregano
1   teaspoon vinegar

Remove tops and seeds from green peppers, clean well and drain. In a large bowl and using a fork, thoroughly mix the beef and ham, and add onion, garlic, oregano, pepper, cumin and salt. Mix in one well-beaten egg to the mixture.

In a small bowl, beat the remaining egg well and add the flour to egg to make a paste. Fill green peppers with the meat mixture until they are almost full. Then fill in the top with the paste-like mixture.

In a deep skillet, heat the cooking oil and place green peppers top side down for a minute or two until the paste topping is golden brown. Remove peppers.

In another skillet, make the sauce by cooking onion and garlic in the olive oil. Add tomato sauce, wine, water, oregano, and vinegar. Lay peppers on their sides in the deep skillet and pour sauce over them. Cook on one side about 20 minutes, then turn carefully and cook on the other side about 10 minutes or until meat inside is done. Serve with fluffy white rice.

Serves 6.

SHRIMP IN TOMATO SAUCE
Enchilado de Camarones

1	pound fresh jumbo shrimp
¼	cup pure Spanish olive oil
1	tablespoon minced garlic
½	onion, finely chopped
½	green bell pepper, finely chopped
1½	teaspoons vinegar
1	6-ounce can tomato paste
1	teaspoon oregano
1	bay leaf
½	cup dry white wine
¾	cup water reserved from the boiling shrimp
	Salt to taste
	Cooked white rice for 4 persons

Boil shrimp for 3 minutes and clean. Reserve ¾ cup of the water the shrimp was boiled in. In a deep frying pan, heat olive oil. Add garlic, onion and green pepper. Cook the mixture until onion is translucent. Add vinegar, tomato paste, oregano, bay leaf, wine, and shrimp water. Mix well and cook over medium heat until mixture begins to bubble. Reduce heat to a simmer. Add shrimp just prior to serving and mix well. Serve over white rice.

Serves 2-3.

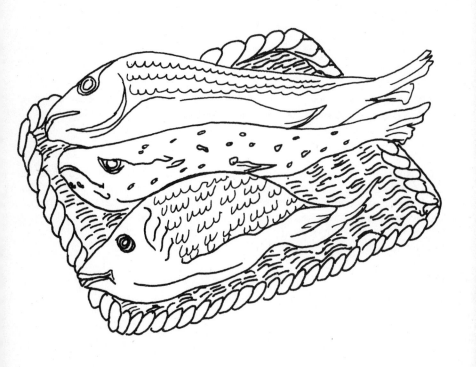

PAELLA

This special dish is similar to Chicken and Yellow Rice. Some variations are made with seafood and pork, seafood and chicken, rabbit, sausage and a variety of ingredients. Use all or some of the following: fish, lobster, shrimp, clams, oysters. Be sure to clean and pre-cook all seafood and remove from shells. Reserve liquid after boiling.

Follow recipe for Chicken and Yellow Rice (on page 37), except use water reserved from cooking seafood. Add seafood to rice just prior to serving, and mix well.

To serve, heap Paella on a large platter and garnish with asparagus, preferably white, tiny sweet peas, and pimiento strips. An attractive presentation is made by surrounding the platter of Paella with raw oysters on the half-shell.

Serves 4.

PAELLA VALENCIANA

½   cup olive oil
1   medium onion, chopped
1   green bell pepper, chopped
½   cup ripe tomatoes, peeled and chopped
3   cloves garlic, minced
1   whole bay leaf
½   pound pork, cut into 1" chunks
½   fryer chicken, cut into 4 pieces
1   pound lobster meat, cut into chunks
½   pound shrimp, peeled and deveined
8   oysters, shucked
8   scallops
8   mussels
4   clams with shells scrubbed and intact
4   stone crab claws
1   pound red snapper, cut into chunks
3   cups fish stock, chicken stock or bottled clam juice
    Few threads of saffron
1   teaspoon salt
1½ cups uncooked white rice
¼   cup white wine
1   can petit green peas, for garnish
1   can asparagus, for garnish
1   jar pimientos, for garnish.

Preheat oven to 350° F.

Pour olive oil into a large paella pan. Add onions and peppers and fry until just limp. Add tomatoes, garlic and bay leaf and cook for about 5 minutes. Add pork and chicken and sauté until tender, stirring to prevent sticking or burning.

Add seafood, fish stock, saffron and salt to taste. When mixture comes to a boil add rice. Stir and bring to a second boil. Cover and bake in oven for about 20 minutes, being careful not to overcook the seafood.

To serve, sprinkle with wine and garnish with peas, asparagus and pimiento.

From THE COLUMBIA RESTAURANT, TAMPA, FLORIDA

Serves 4.

CODFISH A LA BASQUE
Bacalao a la Vizcaina
(Allow Time For Salted Cod To Soak)

1   pound boneless salted codfish, or fresh boneless codfish (4 fillets)
2   tablespoons pure Spanish olive oil
1   large potato, cut into ¼-inch slices
2   cups Sofrito (see page 87)
¼   cup dry white Sherry or other white wine
½   cup water
1   2-ounce jar pimiento strips
     Cooked white rice for 4 persons

If using dried salted codfish, you must soak it for 18 hours, frequently changing the water. Afterwards, put fish in fresh water and simmer until tender (about 30 minutes). Sample a flake of the fish to determine if it is still too salty. If so, change water again to fresh water and cook a bit longer. When the fish is no longer salty, remove from water, allow to cool, and separate into 4 pieces, if not already separated.

In a deep frying pan, add 2 tablespoons of olive oil and arrange potato slices in a layer. Layer the fish (either the prepared salted, or fresh) over the potatoes. In a separate bowl, mix Sofrito, wine, and water and pour over fish and potatoes. Cover and cook for about 20 minutes on medium-low heat until potatoes are tender and fish is done. Sprinkle pimiento strips on top. Serve with white rice.

Serves 4.

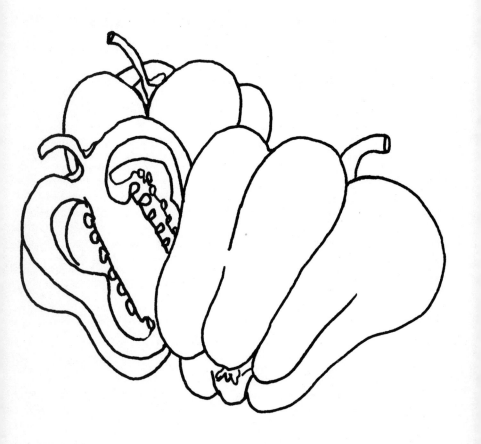

BAKED FISH
Pescado Asado

1   4- to 6-pound fresh whole fish
2   large potatoes, thinly sliced
1   tablespoon minced fresh garlic
1   lemon, juiced (or juice of ½ sour orange)
¼   cup dry white Sherry or other white wine
¼   cup pure Spanish olive oil
1   green pepper, sliced into rings
1   large onion, sliced into rings

Preheat oven to 350° F. Begin with the whole fish (including head and tail). Clean and scale. Fresh snapper, yellowtail, grouper or similar types of fish, approximately 4-6 pounds in size, will serve about 4 people.

Place potato slices on the bottom of a baking dish large enough to accommodate the fish. Make a few slices in the skin of the fish and place fish over the potatoes. Mix together garlic, juice, wine and oil, and pour over fish. Arrange the green pepper and onion slices on top of fish. Bake uncovered at 350°F. until it is done. You will know it is done when a knife carefully inserted and pulled aside reveals a flaky fish. Do not overcook. Serve whole on a decorative platter.

Serves 4.

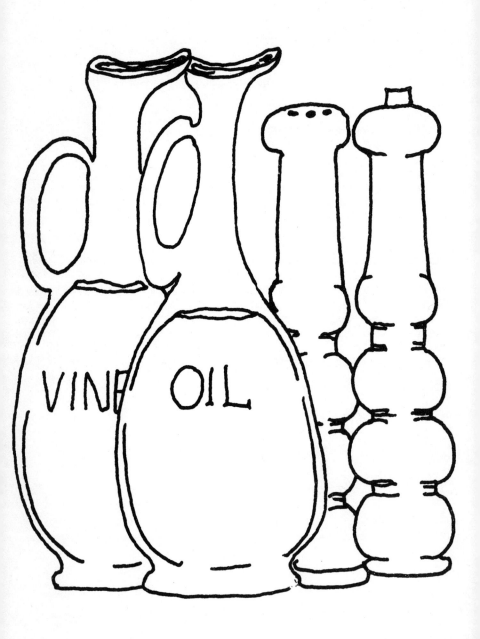

SQUID AND RICE
Arroz con Calamares

1	teaspoon fresh minced garlic
1	onion, finely chopped
¼	green bell pepper, finely chopped
½	dried hot red pepper
¼	cup pure Spanish olive oil
1	can (about 4 ounces) squid, with or without ink
¼	cup tomato sauce
1	tablespoon vinegar
3	cups water
2	cups Valencia rice

Cook garlic, onion, and green pepper, and hot red pepper in olive oil for about 1 minute. Add squid, and ink (if desired), tomato sauce,, and vinegar and cook several minutes. Mix this sauce with the water and add to the rice in another saucepan. Cook undisturbed and covered over medium-low heat for about 15 to 20 minutes until rice is tender and liquid is absorbed. Mix and fluff rice. Serve while hot.

Serves 4.

MOJO SEASONING SAUCE
Mojo

3	tablespoons pure Spanish olive oil, heated
2	tablespoons finely chopped onion
2	garlic cloves, minced
½	teaspoon ground oregano
¼	teaspoon ground cumin
	Dash ground bay leaves
	Dash black pepper
⅛	teaspoon salt
2	tablespoons sour orange or lime juice
2	tablespoons water
1	tablespoon Sherry wine
½	teaspoon vinegar

Mix the onion and garlic, along with the spices, salt, and pepper in a bowl, and then add to a pan with the heated olive oil. Cook just until onion becomes translucent, and then add juice, water, wine and vinegar and simmer about 5 minutes. Allow to cool slightly before serving.

Yields ½ cup.

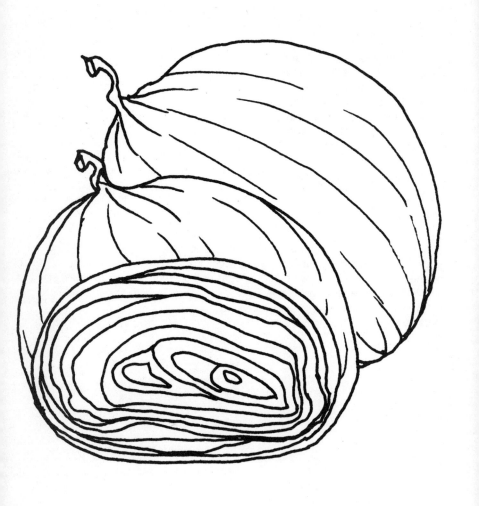

SOFRITO SEASONING SAUCE
Sofrito

¼   cup pure Spanish olive oil
1   tablespoon minced garlic
1   medium onion, finely chopped
½   green bell pepper, finely chopped
½   cup tomato sauce
¼   cup water
⅛   teaspoon ground oregano
¼   teaspoon salt to taste
2   teaspoons vinegar

Cook garlic, onion, and green pepper in olive oil until the onions are translucent. Add remaining ingredients and cook over medium-low heat for about 5 minutes. Store tightly in refrigerator.

Yields 1 cup.

CUBAN SANDWICH
Sandwich Cubano

1	large loaf Cuban bread
1	pound smoked ham, thinly sliced
1	pound roast pork, thinly sliced
½	pound salami, thinly sliced (optional)
½	pound Swiss cheese, sliced and julienned
10-12	pickle slices
	Lettuce and sliced tomatoes (optional)
	Mustard
	Mayonnaise or butter

Cut bread into quarters, about a foot long each. Slice open lengthwise and place ham, pork, and salami in layers along one-half of the sliced loaf. Spread Swiss cheese along length of sandwich and add pickle slices. Add lettuce and tomato slices.

Spread both sides of loaf with mustard and mayonnaise to taste, and close sandwich. Warm for a minute or two to toast the outside of the bread nice and toasty. This is easily done on a grill with lid.

From the SILVER RING CAFE, YBOR CITY, TAMPA, FLORIDA

Serves 4.

BAKED CUSTARD
Flan

1	14-ounce can sweetened condensed milk
½	cup milk
½	cup water
4	egg yolks, well beaten
1	teaspoon pure vanilla extract

Preheat oven to 350° F. Mix all ingredients together in a large bowl and pour into a 1½-quart baking dish that has been lined with a dark, golden-brown caramel coating (see Diplomatic Pudding for instructions, page 97).

Place pan in a larger pan that contains water and bake at 350° F. for about 55-65 minutes, or until pudding is softly set. Remove baking pan from pan of water, allow to cool, and refrigerate until the custard is well chilled.

Set chilled dish in a pan of warm water for a few minutes making sure custard is free from the dish. Invert onto a platter. Cut and serve with drizzles of the caramel spooned on top.

Serves 6.

CUSTARD
Natilla

3   cups milk
½   lemon rind
1   cinnamon stick
4   tablespoons cornstarch
¼   cup water
½   cup sugar
4   egg yolks
1   teaspoon pure vanilla extract
    Pinch of ground fresh cinnamon

In a small saucepan, heat 1 cup milk, lemon rind, and cinnamon stick until boiling. Remove from heat. Dissolve cornstarch in the water. In a large saucepan, mix the remaining cold milk and cornstarch solution.

Mix sugar and egg yolks together and slowly stir into cold milk. Strain the cup of hot milk to remove lemon rind, cinnamon stick, and any particles. Now add hot milk to cold-milk mixture, and heat over medium heat until thick. Stir constantly, and remove from heat when thickened. Add vanilla extract and mix well. Allow to cool enough to pour into individual serving cups. Sprinkle tops wih cinnamon and refrigerate until chilled.

Serves 4.

BACON FROM HEAVEN
Tocino del Cielo

1	cup sugar
½	cup water
9	egg yolks, well-beaten
1	teaspoon pure vanilla extract
1½	quart baking dish or 6 custard cups
	Caramel Lining (see recipe Diplomatic Pudding, page 97)

Preheat oven to 350° F. Prepare a syrup by mixing sugar and water in a small saucepan, and bring to boil for several minutes until sugar is dissolved. Add syrup to well-beaten egg yolks. Add vanilla extract and mix well. Pour mixture into caramel-lined baking dish or custard cups.

Set in a pan filled with water and bake for about 50 to 60 minutes. Remove from pan of water. Cool custard and refrigerate until chilled. To serve, invert on a platter or serving dish that has been lightly greased with butter or margarine.

This is a sweet dish that has bacon only in its name!

Serves 6.

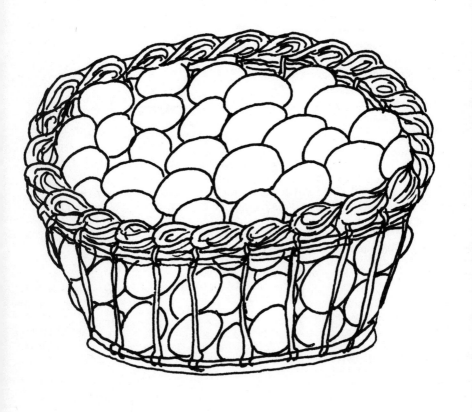

DIPLOMATIC PUDDING
Pudín Diplomatico

Carmel-Coated Baking Dish

½ cup granulated sugar
1 tablespoon unsalted butter
2 tablespoons water

Mix ingredients in a small saucepan and cook on medium to medium-high heat, stirring until mixture begins to bubble and turns a caramel brown. Be very careful not to burn.

Pour hot caramel into a 1½-quart pre-warmed baking dish. Holding the dish with potholders. Roll hot caramel around dish to coat sides. Set aside to cool.

Pudding

3 slices white bread with crust removed
1 14-ounce can sweetened condensed milk
¾ cup water
¼ teaspoon baking powder
3 egg yolks, well-beaten
1 tablespoon vermouth
1 tablespoon flour
1 teaspoon pure vanilla extract
1 6-ounce can fruit cocktail, drained.

Preheat oven to 350° F. In a large bowl, crumble the bread and mix with milk, water, baking powder, egg yolks, vermouth, flour, and vanilla extract. Mix drained fruit cocktail into the batter. Pour mixture into the caramel-coated baking dish.

Set baking dish in a pan of water and bake at 350° F. for 50 minutes or until a toothpick when inserted comes out clean. Remove dish from pan of water and chill. To serve, invert dish onto platter and slice.

Serves 6.

BREAD PUDDING
Pudín de Pan

¼	pound white bread (about 7 slices)
1½	cups milk
1	cup sugar
¼	teaspoon cinnamon
3	eggs
½	cup self-rising flour
1	teaspoon pure vanilla extract
3	tablespoons melted butter or margarine
¼	teaspoon baking powder
½	cup raisins
¼	cup toasted slivered almonds

In a large bowl, remove crust from bread, crumble and pour the milk over bread. Mix in sugar, cinnamon, eggs, flour, vanilla extract, butter and baking powder. Mix well. Add raisins and toasted almonds.

Turn into 1½-quart baking pan lined with butter and bake at 350° F. for 45-55 minutes. (The pudding should have a consistency between that of a pudding and a heavy cake.) Allow to cool, then slice and serve with a small amount of Anise Syrup (recipe follows) poured over the top.

Serves 8.

Anise Syrup

½	cup sugar
¼	cup water
2	tablespoons light corn syrup
2-3	drops anise extract

Mix sugar and water in a small saucepan and boil, constantly stirring until sugar dissolves. Simmer until the liquid becomes clear, then add corn syrup and anise extract.

Yields ½ cup.

COCONUT BALLS
Coquitos

1	18- ounce can grated coconut in heavy syrup*
2	tablespoons brown sugar
1	teaspoon pure vanilla extract
½	cup white sugar

Drain syrup from coconut. Mix coconut, brown sugar, and vanilla together in a medium-size saucepan and cook over medium heat for a few minutes. Allow mixure to cool and then form into small balls (about one inch in diameter). Place balls about one inch apart on a buttered cookie sheet and refrigerate while making the coating.

To prepare coating, mix coconut syrup and white sugar in a small saucepan and cook over medium-high heat, stirring frequently until it becomes a chocolate brown. Spoon over the balls, completely covering them, and allow them to cool. The syrup coating should be brittle while the inside coconut should be tender.

Yield: 12 coquitos

*Available at most Cuban or Spanish markets.

CUBAN COFFEE
Café Cubano

There are three basic ways Cuban coffee is served:
1) EXPRESSO COFFEE. (Café Cubano)
    served in a demitasse cup of 2 to 2½ ounces.
2) COFFEE AND MILK. (Café con Leche)
    served in a regular coffee cup with saucer.
3) CORTADITO. Equivalent to cappucino,
    served in a small glass or cappucino cup of 4 to 6 ounces.

Many years ago water was boiled and poured over the ground coffee in small cloth bags. With the introduction of Italian-made machines, preparing coffee is much simpler. Now, hot water, using steam pressure, is forced through finely ground dark roasted coffee. You can purchase the popular small stovetop espresso maker such as Cubans have been using in their homes for many years. Electric automatic espresso-cappucino makers are also very convenient.

ESPRESSO COFFEE
Café Cubano

If you have an electric espresso maker, follow the manufacturer's directions. If you have a small stovetop espresso coffee maker (and did not receive any directions) prepare your coffee in the following manner:

1) Fill lower chamber with water almost up to the little steam valve.
2) Fill basket with dark roasted coffee specifically ground for espresso coffee. Set basket at top of lower chamber.
3) Tightly screw on the top chamber and set coffee pot on stove. Brew on medium-high heat until bubbling sound stops and coffee is no longer filling top chamber. Remove from heat.
4) Pour coffee into demitasse cup about ⅔ cup full and add sugar to taste (about 1½ teaspoons).
5) Mix well by spoon or use small battery-operated coffee mixer to produces a desirable frothy top on the coffee. Serve immediately. Leftover coffee may be covered and refrigerated to be used in Café con Leche (recipe follows).

COFFEE AND MILK
Café con Leche

1) Heat whole milk in the amount equivalent to number of cups to be served. Heat just until it begins to boil.

2) Pour milk immediately into coffee cups and add espresso coffee as desired, about 2 tablespoons.

3) Sweeten coffee with sugar to taste.

Café con Leche is often served at breakfast with buttered Cuban toasted bread, and at other times during the day as well.

ESPRESSO AND MILK
Cortadito

1) Heat one demitasse cup of whole milk and one demitasse cup of previously made espresso together in a small saucepan. You may not need to heat the espresso if just freshly made.

2) When it begins to boil, remove from heat and pour into cup or small heat-resistant glass of 4-6 ounces.

3) Add sugar to taste and serve hot.

ELEPHANT STEW, CUBAN STYLE
Caldo de Elefante

This is a Cuban version of a popular school recipe.

1   elephant, medium size, obtained legally
1   barrel garlic cloves, finely minced
1   crate sour oranges, squeezed
1   barrel salt
2   chickens (optional)

Cut elephant into bite-size pieces. (It is reported to take about two weeks.) Work garlic into the meat well. Cook over a kerosene stove for 4 days at 450° F. Sprinkle with sour orange juice and salt.

This recipe will serve 3,800 people for lunch. If you run short of food, add the two chickens. If seating is a problem, you may invite 1,000 people for four days (some may want to come twice), but most importantly – be sure to keep everything properly refrigerated!

GLOSSARY

BIJOL
Ground annatto seed which is used to make a condiment which gives rice and soup a yellow color with some subtle flavoring. "Bija-Bekal" is a brand-name product used in the same manner as bijol, although it consists of Spanish paprika, yellow and red colorings and spices.

BONIATO
Cuban sweet potato that is similar to the sweet potato in taste but not as sweet. The flesh is white or yellow, and the skin is mottled. Rock-hard tubers are best.

CALABAZA
Cuban squash which is pumpkin-like and is rarely smaller than a honeydew. Calabaza consists of a fine-grained orange flesh. In recipes calling for calabaza, pumpkin may be substituted, and if it is a sweet recipe, more sugar may be needed.

CAPERS
A green unopened flower of the caper bush. Usually packed in jars with vinegar and salt.

CASSAVA
The tuber-shaped root of the cassava plant. The flesh is white and the bark is dark, measuring about 2 inches wide by 8-10 inches long. Of the two varieties (one sweet and one bitter), use the sweet variety for boiling.

CUMIN
An herb used as one of the major ingredients in curry and chili powder. It is often added to bean soups, meat dishes and many other Hispanic dishes..

CONGRI
Red kidney beans (frijoles colorados) and white rice cooked together with seasonings.

FLAN
A custard made with eggs, milk, sugar, and vanilla extract. There are many varieties: such as coconut, pineapple, and calabaza, with liqueurs occasionally added.

MALANGA
A starchy tuber with a shaggy brown skin and shaped like a sweet potato.

MOROS
Black beans (frijoles negros) and white rice cooked together with seasonings.

NATILLA
A custard-like pudding.

OREGANO
A very aromatic herb consisting of the leaves of the oregano plant, especially good in tomato sauces.

PALOMILLA
A thin cut of top sirloin steak very popular in the Hispanic community.

PICADILLO
A spicy meat dish composed of ground beef, ham, and sometimes pork with chopped vegetables and seasonings.

PLANTAIN
A member of the banana family. The ripe plantain may be fried or boiled after the peel is removed. The unripe plantains are generally peeled, cut, and fried. Plantains are not eaten raw. Ripe (sweet) plantains are soft and orange-yellow inside, with partially black or all-black peels. Unripe plantains are green, and they may be ripened by placing in a brown paper bag for several days.

SAFFRON
Dried stigmas of the saffron plant. They are used to produce a yellow-orange color to dishes, have a rich, briny flavor.

SOFRITO
A tomato sauce seasoned with herbs and spices, as well as onion and green pepper sautéed in olive oil. The name Sofrito means "fried a little."

SOUR ORANGE
Also known as bitter orange, it is much more pungent than the sweet orange. To approximate the sour orange juice taste, use half sweet .orange juice and half lime or lemon juice.

SPANISH OLIVE OIL
Olive oil prepared with Spanish olives. The flavor is distinctive and of excellent quality.

TASAJO
Dried cured beef.

TOCINO DEL CIELO
The literal translation is "bacon from heaven." It is similar to flan but contains no milk and no bacon!

VALENCIA STYLE RICE
A short-grain rice preferred over long-grain rice in dishes like "Paella" and "Arroz con Pollo."

VERMICELLI
A wheat flour product similar to spaghetti but thinner. It is of Italian origin, with the name meaning "little worms."

VINO SECO
This literally means "dry wine," usually referring to dry white wine. Dry white cooking wines produced and bottled in Spain with a 1½% salt content are often referred to casually as "vino seco."

SEASIDE ORDER FORM

Name _____

Address _____

Ship to
Address _____

City, State, Zip _____
Day Phone ( ) _____

City, State, Zip _____
Day Phone ( ) _____

Title	Price	Qty
Clarita's Cocina	19.95	
¡Cuba Cocina!	25.00	
Cuban Home Cooking	10.95	
Cuisine of Cathay	29.95	
Easygoing Entertaining	18.95	
Favorite Recipes Index	9.95	
International Light Cuisine	24.95	
Slim and Healthy Italian	10.95	
Southern Entertaining	14.95	
Tampa	12.95	
Tropic Cooking	14.95	
Classic Conch Cooking	5.95	
Country Cookin'	11.95	
Guide to Florida's Best Rest.	11.95	
Key Lime Cookin'	5.95	
Real Key Lime Gift Pack	16.99	
Key Lime Desserts	5.95	
Recipes From Orange Grove	5.95	
Restaurants, Recipes, & Res.	14.95	
Seafood!	14.95	
Seafood Recipes	5.95	
Seminole Indian Recipes	5.95	
Underwater Gourmet II	15.95	
How To Swirl, Sniff.. . . Wine	7.95	
Charlotte Herbert's Cookery	8.95	

TROPIC COOKING KEY LIME JUICE
24 8 oz. Bottles

_____ Case(s) @
$59.76 = _____

Sub-Total _____

Shipping **$5.00**

Total _____

Unconditional 30-day money-back guarantee. Pricing and availability are subject to change without notice.

SEASIDE ORDER FORM

Name _____

Address _____

City, State, Zip _____

Day Phone ( ) _____

Ship to

Address _____

City, State, Zip _____

Day Phone ( ) _____

Title	Price	Qty
Clarita's Cocina	19.95	
¡Cuba Cocina!	25.00	
Cuban Home Cooking	10.95	
Cuisine of Cathay	29.95	
Easygoing Entertaining	18.95	
Favorite Recipes Index	9.95	
International Light Cuisine	24.95	
Slim and Healthy Italian	10.95	
Southern Entertaining	14.95	
Tampa	12.95	
Tropic Cooking	14.95	
Classic Conch Cooking	5.95	
Country Cookin'	11.95	
Guide to Florida's Best Rest.	11.95	
Key Lime Cookin'	5.95	
Real Key Lime Gift Pack	16.99	
Key Lime Desserts	5.95	
Recipes From Orange Grove	5.95	
Restaurants, Recipes, & Res.	14.95	
Seafood!	14.95	
Seafood Recipes	5.95	
Seminole Indian Recipes	5.95	
Underwater Gourmet II	15.95	
How To Swirl, Sniff, . . . Wine	7.95	
Charlotte Herbert's Cookery	8.95	

KEY LIME JUICE

TROPIC
COOKING KEY
LIME JUICE
24 8 oz. Bottles

_____ Case(s) @
$59.76 = _____

Sub-Total _____

Shipping **$5.00**

Total _____

Unconditional 30-day money-back guarantee. Pricing and availablity are subject to change without notice.

SEASIDE ORDER FORM

Name _____

Address _____

Ship to
Address _____

City, State, Zip _____
Day Phone ( ) _____

City, State, Zip _____
Day Phone ( ) _____

KEY LIME JUICE

Title	Price	Qty
Clarita's Cocina	19.95	
¡Cuba Cocina!	25.00	
Cuban Home Cooking	10.95	
Cuisine of Cathay	29.95	
Easygoing Entertaining	18.95	
Favorite Recipes Index	9.95	
International Light Cuisine	24.95	
Slim and Healthy Italian	10.95	
Southern Entertaining	14.95	
Tampa	12.95	
Tropic Cooking	14.95	
Classic Conch Cooking	5.95	
Country Cookin'	11.95	
Guide to Florida's Best Rest.	11.95	
Key Lime Cookin'	5.95	
Real Key Lime Gift Pack	16.99	
Key Lime Desserts	5.95	
Recipes From Orange Grove	5.95	
Restaurants, Recipes, & Res.	14.95	
Seafood!	14.95	
Seafood Recipes	5.95	
Seminole Indian Recipes	5.95	
Underwater Gourmet II	15.95	
How To Swirl, Sniff. . . Wine	7.95	
Charlotte Herbert's Cookery	8.95	

TROPIC
COOKING KEY
LIME JUICE
24 8 oz. Bottles

_____ Case(s) @

$59.76 = _____

Sub-Total _____

Shipping **$5.00**

Total _____

Unconditional 30-day money-back guarantee. Pricing and availablity are subject to change without notice.

SEASIDE ORDER FORM

Name _____

Address _____

City, State, Zip _____

Day Phone ( ) _____

Ship to

Address _____

City, State, Zip _____

Day Phone ( ) _____

Title	Price	Qty
Clarita's Cocina	19.95	
¡Cuba Cocina!	25.00	
Cuban Home Cooking	10.95	
Cuisine of Cathay	29.95	
Easygoing Entertaining	18.95	
Favorite Recipes Index	9.95	
International Light Cuisine	24.95	
Slim and Healthy Italian	10.95	
Southern Entertaining	14.95	
Tampa	12.95	
Tropic Cooking	14.95	
Classic Conch Cooking	5.95	
Country Cookin'	11.95	
Guide to Florida's Best Rest.	11.95	
Key Lime Cookin'	5.95	
Real Key Lime Gift Pack	16.99	
Key Lime Desserts	5.95	
Recipes From Orange Grove	5.95	
Restaurants, Recipes, & Res.	14.95	
Seafood!	14.95	
Seafood Recipes	5.95	
Seminole Indian Recipes	5.95	
Underwater Gourmet II	15.95	
How To Swirl, Sniff.. . . Wine	7.95	
Charlotte Herbert's Cookery	8.95	

TROPIC COOKING KEY LIME JUICE
24 8 oz. Bottles

___ Case(s) @
$59.76 = _____

Sub-Total _____

Shipping **$5.00**

Total _____

REMEMBER
Cookbooks make great gifts for people of all ages.

send orders to:

Seaside

687 Alderman Road #203
Palm Harbor, Florida 34683
1-888-Fla-Book (352-2665)

Make checks payable to:

Seaside

Thank you for
your order.

Unconditional 30-day money-back guarantee. Pricing and availability are subject to change without notice.

SEASIDE ORDER FORM

Name _____
Address _____

City, State, Zip _____
Day Phone ( ) _____

Ship to
Address _____

City, State, Zip _____
Day Phone ( ) _____

send orders to:

Seaside

687 Alderman Road #203
Palm Harbor, Florida 34683
1-888-Fla-Book (352-2665)

Make checks payable to:
Seaside

Thank you for
your order.

**TROPIC
COOKING KEY
LIME JUICE
24 8 oz. Bottles**

_____ Case(s) @
$59.76 = _____

Title	Price	Qty
Clarita's Cocina	19.95	
¡Cuba Cocina!	25.00	
Cuban Home Cooking	10.95	
Cuisine of Cathay	29.95	
Easygoing Entertaining	18.95	
Favorite Recipes Index	9.95	
International Light Cuisine	24.95	
Slim and Healthy Italian	10.95	
Southern Entertaining	14.95	
Tampa	12.95	
Tropic Cooking	14.95	
Classic Conch Cooking	5.95	
Country Cookin'	11.95	
Guide to Florida's Best Rest.	11.95	
Key Lime Cookin'	5.95	
Real Key Lime Gift Pack	16.99	
Key Lime Desserts	5.95	
Recipes From Orange Grove	5.95	
Restaurants, Recipes, & Res.	14.95	
Seafood!	14.95	
Seafood Recipes	5.95	
Seminole Indian Recipes	5.95	
Underwater Gourmet II	15.95	
How To Swirl, Sniff,. . . Wine	7.95	
Charlotte Herbert's Cookery	8.95	

Sub-Total _____

Shipping **$5.00**

Total _____

Unconditional 30-day money-back guarantee. Pricing and availablity are subject to change without notice.

Publishing

687 Alderman Road #203
Palm Harbor, Florida 34683
1-888-Fla-Book (352-2665)